Be ████████ ears

Our world

Smo1006537
8/02
£12-95
910.7
(Alc)

Kathy Alcock

0947882456

Acknowledgements

The author and the publisher would like to thank the following for their invaluable help and support during the preparation of this book:

Amanda Symonds	Helen McMorrow	Shelagh Hughes
Carol Thurman	Isabelle Dillon	Stephen Scoffham
Chris Alcock	Janet Parrett	Stuart Alcock
Christine Laxton	Jill Marsh	Sue Birbeck
Debbie Galley-Buxton	John Collar	Sue Brown
Denise Hill	Laura Christie	Sue Smith
Elizabeth Barber	Lynne Gibbon	Sue Woolgar
Elizabeth Crosson	Marc Barber	Tina Wallace
Fiona Johnston	Mary Letham	Tracy Green
Hania Myers	Nicola Hooper	Victor Parrett
Hardip Banger	Philip Alcock	Warren Harrison
Heather Woodcock	Sarah Newbrook	

Thank you also to the children, students and parents in the following:

Abbey Pre-School	South Deal Primary School
Archers Court School	St Mary's C.E.P. School
Canterbury Christ Church University College	The Parochial School
Hamilton School	Umbrella Pre-school
River C.P. School	Warden House School
Sandwich Infants School	Whitfield Community Playgroup

Freelance Publisher and Designer: Patricia Harrison
Design and page layout: Ed Gallagher   **Cover design:** Martin Cross, Ed Gallagher
Photography: Kelvin Freeman, Steve Harrison and Canterbury Christ Church College

First published in 2001 by Belair Publications.
Reprinted 2002

ISBN 0 94788 245 6

Contents

Introduction	4
Through the window	6
Over the rainbow	8
Out and about	10
Out for a walk	12
How we travel around	14
Over land and sea	16
Reasons why we travel	18
Let's communicate	20
How we communicate	22
Who will you ring?	24
Whatever the weather	26
What's the weather like today?	28
The seasons	30
All the year round	32
Hot and cold places	34
Dough corner and clay square	36
Clay displays and collections	38
On the farm	40
The world of fairy tales	42
Compass town	46
The street where you live	48
The world where we live	50
Where in the world?	52
Where should we go?	54
Far and away places	56
Jobs people do	58
In the park	60
Action songs and rhymes	62

We found out about rainforests

Introduction

The aim of this series is to provide resource material covering all the main areas of young children's learning. Each book is a 64 page full colour resource, which provides practical 'hands on' activities suitable for working with under-fives. They also provide a variety of starting points to encourage and promote creative play.

Written by professionals working in early years education, each book is organised into popular early years themes, providing ideas to develop the six areas of learning identified in the **Curriculum guidance for the foundation stage.**

These are:

- **Personal, social and emotional development;**
- **Communication, language and literacy;**
- **Mathematical development;**
- **Knowledge and understanding of the world;**
- **Physical development;**
- **Creative development;**

In the area of learning '**Knowledge and understanding of the world**' children develop the knowledge, skills and understanding to help them make sense of the world. This forms the foundation for children's later work in science, design and technology, history, geography and information and communication technology (ICT). The foundation stage for future work in geography in this area of learning involves children developing a sense of place

The 'Early learning goals for a sense of place' are:

- **Observe, find out and identify features in the place they live and in the natural world.**
- **Find out about their environment, and talk about those features they like and dislike.**

For children in their early years, the variety within the human and natural world can cause confusions. Their experiences are limited but even within their first few years of life, children meet large numbers of different people and some children will visit a wide variety of different places though every day experiences. This book demonstrates ways in which these experiences can be built upon to provide relevant, stimulating, interesting and enjoyable learning activities to enable them to 'make sense of the world'.

The **Curriculum guidance for the foundation stage** identifies what '**effective learning and teaching**' requires within the field of '**Knowledge and understanding of the world**'.

Practical Activities

Children learn by 'doing things' and by working with a range of materials. Some readers will have access to more facilities and resources than others. This book is full of practical activities for you to select from and it aims to provide something for everyone, from a parent or carer at home to a fully equipped Nursery school or Reception class.

Interaction with each other and with adults

Children learn by hearing new words and imitating adults. Each of the themes in this book includes ideas of how adults should interact with children.

Gathering information

Children need opportunities to collect information to satisfy their curiosity about the world around them. An excellent way of doing this is by taking children on visits. In this book you will find ideas about what to do **before, during and after visits** in order to maximise the potential learning that can take place.

Practitioners teaching powerful lesson by modelling different behaviour

Children learn how to investigate, ask questions, use reference skills, and solve problems, by seeing and listening to adults operate in this way. It is important to 'model' for the children the behaviour you want them to learn.

Direct teaching of skills and knowledge

There are times when you will need to give the children information, this should be planned for example, on how to behave on a visit to ensure safety or how to use equipment. There are other times when giving information can stifle investigation and the sense of wonder when a discovery is made. For example by telling the children how the cows are milked, prior to a farm visit.

Practitioners who interact with, and support children by encouraging them and helping them learn from their mistakes

Children should be given choices and be encouraged to try out new ideas. If ideas don't work this should not be interpreted as failure but a problem to be solved.

The use of carefully framed questions

Each of the themes in this book includes suggestions of 'Questions to ask' and appropriate language you should be aiming to develop.

Planning for equal access to the curriculum

Adults should give all children the access to all the activities provided.

TALK ABOUT

Questions to ask	Language development
What does this picture show?	Encourage the children to:
Where is it?	name features
What are the people doing?	describe activities
What do you like/ dislike about this place?	pass opinions

Making effective use of outdoors and the local environment

Using the outdoor environment is an essential part of this area of learning. This book includes exciting ideas for providing outdoor experiences that are on a large scale such as construction and mapping and how to extend the outdoor activities during indoor play.

Giving careful consideration to the provision and access of resources

The resources that you will need for the suggested activities are identified at the beginning of each theme.

YOU WILL NEED

- Modelling clay, dough or plasticine
- Rolling pins
- Paint
- Card
- Objects to put in shops
- Biscuits

Home Links

- Ask children to look for plates with pictures on them to bring into class to form a display.
- Assist an adult to make biscuits or cakes.
- Look for ways of using clay in and around the home.
- When shopping with parents, look for different sorts of bread, biscuits and cakes which are for sale.

Using parent's knowledge to extend children's experiences of the world

Ideas of how parents might support the children's learning are included.

The author believes that the greatest resource any teacher or worker with early years children has is their own imagination.
The ideas in this book are designed to stimulate your imagination.

Through the window

LEARNING INTENTIONS

Children will:

- express their ideas pictorially;
- increase their awareness of the features surrounding their school;
- look at the work of famous artists.

YOU WILL NEED

- paint mixed for each colour of the rainbow
- different size brushes
- sugar paper to make window frames
- large pieces of white paper
- pictures of the works of famous artists

STARTING POINTS

- Go for a walk in the local area and talk about the buildings and natural features. Take photographs of features using a digital or Polaroid camera.

- Ask the children to name features they can see through the window.

- Paint pictures of what they can see out of the window, in the playground or park or inside. Take photographs of the actual scene and display near the children's paintings.

- Display paintings by famous artists.

Activities

- Look at the work of a famous artist. Talk about what the picture shows and the techniques used. Ask questions such as: 'What does this painting show?' 'What shapes can you see?' 'What colours has the artist used?'

- Display the children's paintings next to or over the originals to create a 'lift the flap' effect. The work of art used here is Van Gogh's 'Sunflowers'.

- Ask children to paint in a particular style, for example using coloured dots, or soaking sugar paper with clear water then dropping spots of coloured paint on the wet paper, using pastels.

What can you see through your window?

(Display board labels: Jessica; A house and some flowers; Oliver W.; Birds flying; I can see the sun; Lauren; Paris; A big house; I can see the trees; I can see a garden; Sarah)

Activities

✋ Make a list of all the things the children can see.

✋ Provide an outline picture showing the scene children can see from the window. Children add details using their own observations. Make labels for some of the features such as house, garden, tree, sky, road, path, post box. Children attach these labels to the features on the picture.

✋ Play a simplified version of the game 'I spy …' for example: 'I spy something which leaves grow on …'

Questions to ask

What can you see?
What is behind the …?
What is in front of the …?
Can you describe where … is?
I spy ….

Language development

Children name features.
Position language:- *behind, above, beyond, next to, right, left, in front of, beside, across.*

Over the rainbow

Activities

👋 Look at a rainbow when it appears in the sky or a picture of a rainbow.

👋 Teach the children seven colours.

👋 Ask them to paint their own picture of a rainbow.

red orange yellow green blue indigo violet

Children can use thick brushes, or thin brushes, or fingers. Ask them which they think is most effective.

Richard

Of

York

Gained

Battle

In

Vain

Activities

👋 Make a giant class rainbow. This could go over a door as in the photograph.

👋 A giant class rainbow could be the centrepiece of a display of objects relating to a theme such as food, for example, you may have a red apple, an orange, a yellow lemon, a green lettuce, a blue box of biscuits, an indigo plum, a violet packet of sweets. Other themes may include clothes, the weather, animals, toys, objects found in the garden, objects found in the street.

👋 Create a group or class poem on the theme.

Home Links

● Ask parents to contribute to the rainbow display by providing coloured objects.

● Ask parents to encourage their children to look for rainbow colours when they are out and about.

Out and about

LEARNING INTENTIONS

Children will:

- talk about their experiences and increase their awareness of their surroundings;

- increase their awareness of how numbers are used in the environment;

- develop mapwork skills.

STARTING POINTS

- Talk about places and features children pass as they travel to class.

- Use photographs as stimuli in encouraging children to talk about places they have visited with adults.

- Introduce the concept of 'plan view' by making a simple plan of the classroom. Put Velcro on the plan and on the furniture. Children have to place the pieces in the right place.

We park the car here

I could call my mum from here

I had my party here

We can buy stamps here

IMPORTANT NOTE

All the following activities could take place in a rural or urban environment, nearby or further afield. It is essential when taking children out of doors that an appropriate adult/children ratio is achieved. All adult helpers must be suitably prepared in advance to ensure maximum learning from the experience.

People post letters to friends

Before the visit

Identify a place to be visited such as a local park, play area or place of worship. Talk about what the children know already about it. Look at a photograph of what it looks like now and if possible, in the past so changes can be identified. Look at the place on a large-scale map or an aerial photograph.

Prepare speech bubbles to be completed after the visit.

Adults work with children to compile a list of questions to be answered before and during the visit.

Our questions

What is the place called?
Who lives there?
What do people do there?
What buildings are there?
Is it a safe place?
What should people not do there?
What do we like/dislike about the place?

Out for a walk

During the visit

- On the journey, children identify features by completing an 'I have seen…' tally chart.

- During a walk children collect items in a small pot or bag. These can be sorted and displayed on return. (Note: supervise carefully.)

- Stop to take photographs of places children find interesting.

- Play 'I spy' using signs and symbols as well as other easily identified features.

- Children choose a building such as a shop or a house or a feature such as a gate or a bridge and make a close observation by talking into a small portable tape recorder. Photographs of these can be taken and made into a collection. Children listen to the recordings and identify and match to the pictures.

- Ask children to draw or talk about what they can see in front and behind them, or looking down or looking up. North and South may be introduced.

After the visit

- Ask children to identify key features and the route followed on a simple uncomplicated, large-scale map.

- Prepare speech bubbles from card. Children dictate to an adult their comments about places they have visited. Add these to the photographs (see page 11) or to the map display.

- Make signs and symbols for use in the classroom.

- Compare pictures taken of the same place during a different season to look for differences and similarities.

Did you see?

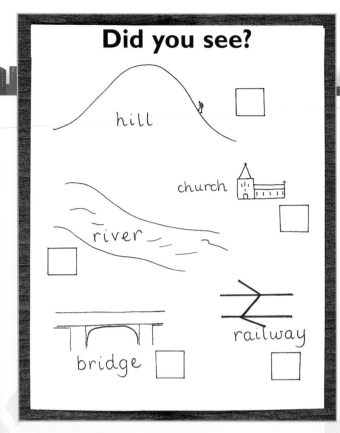

hill

church

river

railway

bridge

Activities

Make a simple symbols chart with a mixture of features they did and did not see. Can the children remember what they saw and where they saw it?

Looking for numbers

Make signs and symbols that you have seen on the visit which use numbers to give information. These may include road signs, dates on buildings, times when cars can be parked and for how long, prices of goods, opening times, car registration numbers.

Make your own versions of these to give information to the children such as opening times for the class shop, prices of food in the class café, the number of children allowed in the book corner or home corner at any one time.

Home Links

- Ask children to talk to adults at home about a visit undertaken.

- Collect pictures of places they would like to find out about.

- Make a car number plate of their own or another car.

- Play number games with the numbers on the plate e.g., add two numbers, order them from largest to smallest.

How we travel around

LEARNING INTENTIONS

Children will:

- distinguish between different forms of transport;

- begin to understand the processes involved in making a journey;

- ask questions about how people travel.

YOU WILL NEED

- computer generated passports for children to complete
- long roll of paper
- assorted paints
- wool for weaving

STARTING POINTS

- Read a story to the children which involves various vehicles and methods of travelling such as one of the Postman Pat, Thomas the Tank Engine or Gumdrop series.

- Visit a train, bus or coach station or an airport.

- Watch vehicles passing the building where you are working. Complete a traffic count.

- A child recounts a journey they have made recently.

- Sing songs such as 'Here comes a big red bus' and 'The Wheels on the Bus'.

- Read 'The Owl and the Pussy Cat' poem by Edward Lear.

ACTIVITIES

✋ Bring in examples of passports. Talk about why people have passports, why they are used and what information they include.

✋ Make a passport and go on a pretend journey abroad. Use the 'magic carpet' or 'all aboard the aeroplane' idea.

✋ Provide tasks for the 'pretend journey' such as:

- Make a place name sign.

- Make a menu for the café.

- Make tickets for the journey.

- Make sound effects for the journey using instruments.

Activities

- Children can make footprints along a long roll of paper.
- Paint the bottom of their feet.
- Carefully supervise them creating footprints.
- Talk to the children about when they might walk on a journey.

- Think about safety.

CROSSING THE ROAD

DO:
stop at the kerb
find an adult
look both ways

DO NOT:
run across the road
stop on the road
play on the road

Activities

- Make footprint instructions.

This can be done in different ways for younger and older children. For children who can read numbers use arrows and numbers e.g., walk forward three paces, right two paces.
For other children use symbols like dots or footprints.

Over land and sea

Activities

- Children paint pictures of journeys across water.
- They could weave wool around the edges of the boat or land in the distance as in this example.
- Talk about where passengers are going and what luggage they would take with them.
- Look at a timetable, make and buy tickets.
- Think of other vehicles that people use and why e.g., buses and cars

BY BOAT

BY TRAIN

Ask the children to act out a journey. Together adults and children create and set out the scene. This could be a train. Children take turns to assume the role of driver, wearing appropriate hat or uniform.

have trave
by bus

BY BUS

Home Links

- Cut out pictures of different vehicles and make a 'How we travel' zig-zag book.

- Ask parents to take a photograph of their child in front of the mode of transport they use when going on a journey.

Questions to ask	**Language development**
Where are you going? How will you travel? How long will it take? When might you travel by bus? plane? train? car?	Holiday, visit, shopping, walk, train, bus, plane, hour, day, long time, town, city, names of places e.g., Spain, London, shopping centre, supermarket.

Reasons why we travel

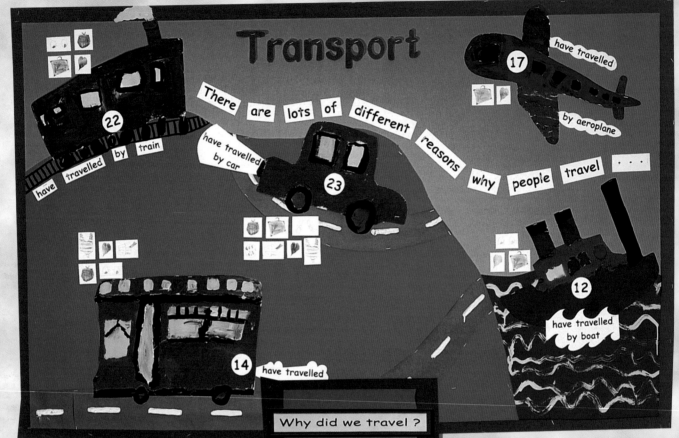

Transport

There are lots of different reasons why people travel ...

22 have travelled by train

have travelled by car

23

17 have travelled by aeroplane

12 have travelled by boat

14 have travelled

Why did we travel ?

	Shopping
	School
	Holiday
	Ballet class
	Visit family
	Football
	Swimming
	Sight seeing

KEY

Asking questions

Who has travelled by car,
(bus, plane, boat)?
Why have you travelled by
car, (bus, plane, boat)?
Which is the best way to
travel if you are going:
on holiday?
to the shops?
to London?
to Sydney?
to New York?

Activities

- Make a simple block graph to
  show how many children
  have travelled on the
  different forms of transport.

- Alternatively put the number
  of children on the form of
  transport as in the collage
  above.

- Ask the children to draw a
  picture that represents the
  reason they travelled. Use
  these as a symbol key for the
  large collage.

Activities

Talk about different types of journeys people make and what luggage they take with them.

Provide a collection of toy vehicles to be sorted into different categories by colour, size, type and what they travel on.

Make a display of vehicles with labels and enquiry questions such as:

What is this?
Where does this travel?
Who travels in this?
How is this used?
How many people could travel in this car?
Where is this bus going to stop?
What is the name of the train station?
Where does the plane fly?
Who travels in a plane?

When children play with toy vehicles, adults talk to them about the scenarios they are creating. Ask questions such as:

When your car crashed why do you think that happened?
Are the people in the coach wearing seat belts?
Where will the ambulance be going?
What is going to happen next?
Where is it safe to cross the road?

Let's communicate

LEARNING INTENTIONS

Children will:

- develop an understanding of communicating for a specific purpose;
- increase awareness of work in a post office;
- engage in role-play.

Miss Polly had a dolly

Miss Polly had a dolly who was sick, sick, sick.
So she called for the doctor to be quick, quick, quick.
The doctor came with his bag and his hat.
And he knocked at the door with a rat-a-tat-tat.

He looked at the dolly and he shook his head,
He said 'Miss Polly, put her straight to bed'.
He wrote on a paper for a pill, pill, pill,
"I'll be back in the morning with my bill, bill, bill."

YOU WILL NEED

- writing materials
- huge box
- paint
- telephones
- office stationery
- sugar paper
- pictures and objects to represent people to call e.g., Lego people.

STARTING POINTS

- Visit a post office where people are working using office equipment.
- Read a story or an information book about one of the emergency services and talk about the work they do and how we communicate with them.
- Sing a song such as 'Miss Polly had a dolly'. (See above.)
- Ask questions such as: 'Why do you use a telephone or fax machine?' 'How do you make a telephone call and what happens?' 'Make and receive a telephone call, a fax message and an email.'

Activities

- Talk about how we communicate with people who do not live nearby.
- Write a letter.
- Make a telephone box in an outdoor area.

Asking questions

Who will you write to?
Where do they live?
What will you write?

What goes on the envelope?

Language development

Names of people they know.
Names of places.
Talk about reasons for writing e.g., Thank you, Birthdays.
Name, address, stamp.

How we communicate

SET UP A POST OFFICE

Activities

- Read 'The Jolly Postman' and the 'Jolly Post Office'.

- Talk to the children about why we need post offices, what services they provide and the jobs people do in them.

- Set up a role play corner - children can play different roles such as postal workers or customers.

- Make labels for the post office.

> **YOU WILL NEED**
> - computer
> - telephone
> - letters
> - parcels
> - scales
> - telephone directories
> - stamps (can be computer generated)
> - toy money

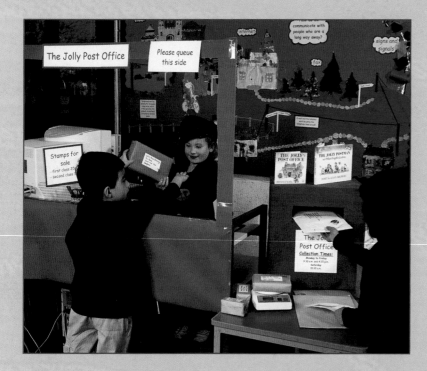

- Make a post box with times of collection displayed.

- Parcels and letters should have local and more distant addresses.

- Make a sorting box with four local streets labelled.

- Children can sort the letters to be delivered to the four streets.

- Make some car tax discs. These can be computer generated by scanning some in.

From over the hills and far away ....

..a jolly postman came one day

How do you send messages to someone who is far away? Do you use the telephone? Do you use e-mail? Do you write letters?

letter

telephone

internet

How do we communicate with people who are a long way away?

signs and signals

fax

Telephones work by sending the messages along wires, which either go under the ground, or overhead attached to wooden poles.

E-mail and the internet work by using the telephone lines as well.

Letters are posted in the post box. They are then collected and taken to the sorting office where they are sent to the town on the address. The postmen and women there deliver the letters to the houses.

Activities

- Ask the children to list all the ways we communicate with people further away for example letter, email, fax, telephone, internet.

- Make a display generated by the ideas in the books.

- Make a display of different types and sizes of letters and parcels, email and faxes.

Home Links

- Ask parents to help their children to generate a short message to send to a relative or friend in another country by email, fax or letter.

Who will you ring?

Activities

👋 Make a giant telephone to use in an interactive display. Create the numbers using materials, which give a tactile effect of spots for counting.

👋 Explain to the children what an emergency call is, how to make the call and when the emergency number should be dialled and when not to dial it.

👋 Use the display to introduce other services which can be contacted by telephone such as a library, shops, schools, post offices, garages, banks, doctors. Talk with the children about what services each provides and where the nearest ones are found.

👋 Add instructions and labels to the telephone display such as:

- Pick up the receiver.
- Hold one end to your ear and the other to your mouth.
- Dial the emergency number.
- Wait for an answer.
- Ask for the service you need.
- Give your name and address.
- Say what the problem is.

Activities

✍ Set up the role play area for the children to use as an office; such as those for an estate agent, car sales, a travel agent or tourist information bureau, a bank, post office, medical centre, or dental surgery.

✍ Equip the office with computer, model and discarded telephones, fax machines and other office equipment with which children experiment. Provide paper, envelopes and different types of writing equipment as well as a waste paper and recycling bin.

Provide a set of task cards relating to the type of area you have set up such as: 'Buy a new house' 'Book a holiday' 'Change some money into Euros'.

Home Links

● Ask parents to take children to visit one or more of the services you have talked and learned about.

● Prepare a short message to send to a friend in another country by email, telephone or fax.

Whatever the weather

LEARNING INTENTIONS

Children will:

- gain a greater understanding of different weather conditions;
- know that there are seasonal patterns to weather e.g., it is more likely to snow in winter;
- know that some places in the world are cold all the time.

Activities

- Cut out the shape of a boy and a girl from cardboard. Provide collections of clothes relating to different types of weather. Fix Velcro to the back of the clothes and in strategic places on the figures. Make title display cards depicting different types of weather.

- Ask the children to dress the boy and the girl appropriately according to the changing weather.

Asking questions	Language development
What is the weather like today?	Hot, cold, cloudy, raining, snowing, windy.
How should we dress the boy and girl today?	Warm clothes, clothes to keep cool.
Hold up an item. When would you wear this?	Name items we wear: in cold weather / in hot weather
What would you wear if the weather was wet, windy etc.?	Hat, jeans, shorts, gloves etc.

Today it is hot

- Change the display to clothes for special occasions or clothes from around the world.

- Use an overhead projector and transparencies.

- Use non-permanent pens to draw the clothes, colour and design them.

pouring

thunderstorm

soaking

Auntie Mabel flew her aeroplane in the pouring rain.

Hannah

splash

thunderstorm

pouring

Lewis

Activities

✍ Write weather words on raindrops.

✍ Children can paint individual pictures of what they, or people they know, do in different weather conditions.

Story map

✍ Make a story map. An adult draws the outline of the scene to be recreated and children select materials to be used to represent each area and feature in the picture.

✍ Create labels and characters with Velcro on the back which children place on appropriate places on a picture map to retell the story of rain.

splash

Oliver W.

The water cycle

A cloud is millions of drops of water.

Clouds are blown by the wind.

When the clouds get too heavy, the drops of water fall as rain.

Water evaporates from trees and plants.

Water runs into rivers.

Water is heated by the sun and evaporates from the sea.

Rivers flow into the sea.

What's the weather like today?

Snow

What clothes do you wear in cold weather?

A Winter Day
By Grace, Mitchell, James and Tamya

Sun

What clothes do you wear in hot weather?

Sunflowers

Wind

What clothes do you wear in windy weather?

A Windy Day
By Daniel, Behr, Sophia and Helen

Thunder and Lightning

What clothes do you wear in stormy weather?

A Scary Storm
By Nathan, Aneeta, Emily and Oliver

Cloud

What clothes do you wear in cloudy weather?

A Cloudy Flight
By Muheen, Luke, Sanum, Ufat and Zeinua

Rain

What clothes do you wear in rainy weather?

Is it Raining?
By Ellie, Sonia, Phillipa, Jack and Eden

Activities

👋 Ask the children to draw weather pictures or contribute to a collage.

👋 Dress the boy and girl appropriately for the weather.

👋 You could laminate some pictures so that the children can draw on the picture with water-based felt tip pens. The example on page 27 asks children to draw raindrops. These can be wiped off easily with a damp cloth for other children to take a turn.

👋 Make a large wall display with your weather pictures around a simple map of the whole country.

👋 Write weather questions on the display for children to answer and talk about.

👋 Make a range of weather symbols for children to put on the map. One for where they live and for other areas. The children can be encouraged to listen to the weather forecast.

Activities

👋 Ask the children to write 'weather words' and draw an appropriate picture.

👋 Make envelopes with the symbols used around the map and use the same words to describe the symbols.

👋 Children put their words in the envelopes which best describes their weather word eg 'nippy' would go in the envelope labelled 'wind'.

The seasons

Activities

👋 Share poems about the seasons.

Asking questions

Do you remember what it was like in

winter?

summer?

autumn?

spring?

What do we wear in summer, autumn, winter and spring? Why?

Language development

Encourage children to think about how seasonal weather affects their lives:

Holidays, building snowmen, kicking fallen leaves.

Sandals, wellingtons, boots, scarves, coats, T-shirts etc.

👋 Make individual collages which represent the seasons.

For example, the sun to represent summer. Let the children choose the materials and colours they will use.

Spring is flowery, bowery, showery

Summer is hoppy, croppy, poppy

Autumn is slippy, drippy, nippy

Winter is breezy, sneezy, freezy

We used these instructions to make our sun visors.

How to make a sun visor

1. Cut a strip of card 60cm long and about 5cm wide.
2. Cut out the peak of the visor by following black lines.
3. Glue peak onto coloured card and cut it out.
4. Fold the peak along the dotted line and staple or sellotape to centre of strip.
5. Decorate the sun visor as you like, then sellotape to fit around head.

Activities

👉 Make a seasonal collage with the focus on colours which the season represents.

Spring	Represent blossom with shades of pink and white and new plants with shades of green.
Summer	Bright, warm, shiny colours such as yellow, gold, red, orange.
Autumn	Dried leaf and seed collages in brown, orange, russet, ochre.
Winter	Colder, darker shades of blue, grey, black, white, silver.

👉 Add appropriate words to the pictures.

Home Links

● Ask children to bring suitable materials for the collage.

● Collect postcards or photographs of different seasons.

● Encourage the parents to talk about what they do in different seasons e.g., summer holidays.

sunrise summer warm sun shadows sunset

sand holidays hot boiling

The sun has got his hat on,
Hip hip hip hooray!

The sun has got his hat on and he's coming out to play.

Would any of these hats keep your head dry?

Which hat would you choose to wear on a sunny day?

Which hat would keep your head warm?

All the year round

- Use photographs of familiar scenes to depict seasonal change throughout the year. Keep the display up all year and add to it as the year progresses.

Summer

Winter

Spring

Autumn

- Talk about the changes that take place and how these affect people's lives.

Remember summer can be hot and wet

Summer

Summer

Cross-curricular links

A seasonal display can also be used for literacy and numeracy development as in the example below.

Which apple is the biggest?

How many green apples can you see on the tree?

Where are the conkers?

How many apples in the basket?

apple prints

The apple tree

Here is a tree with leaves so green.
Here are the apples that hang between
When the wind blows the apples fall
Here is a basket to gather them all

Asking questions

What is the weather like now?

How has it changed since Christmas/ beginning of the year etc?

What kind of clothes do we wear in summer/ winter?

When do people go on holiday if they want hot weather?

Language development

Encourage children to use locational words such as:

above, below, next to, beside, nearer, nearest, right, left

Activities

- Ask children to paint giant leaf shapes for the collage.

- They could collect fallen leaves and also stick these to the collage.

- The collage above has incorporated apple prints.

- Bring in a selection of fruit. Talk about where the fruit is grown. Cut open and look for patterns and seeds. Taste some of the fruit. Ask children to make fruit prints. Can they match the fruit to the print the next day?

Hot and cold places

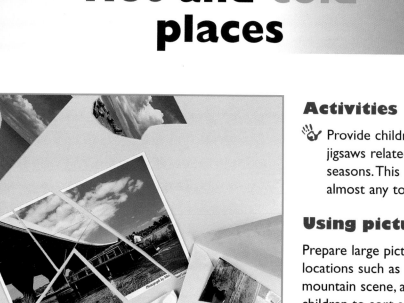

Activities

✋ Provide children with a collection of jigsaws related to the theme of seasons. This idea can relate to almost any topic.

Using pictures

Prepare large pictures of a range of locations such as a beach, a funfair, a mountain scene, a snowscape. Ask children to sort a collection of postcards into trays beneath the pictures.

Collect a range of objects used when it is hot. Make labels e.g., sand, sea etc. as shown in the photograph below. Children pick up an object and select the best place for it e.g., flippers next to the label for sea.

Activities

- Children can make individual snowmen using cotton wool or tissue paper on tubes.

- Teach them the rhyme '10 cold snowmen sitting on the wall', to the tune of '10 Green Bottles'.

- Look at books and pictures of animals in the Artic and Antarctica.

- Use a globe to show the children where these are. They can make different animals to contribute to a collage.

10 cold snowmen sitting on a wall.

The North Pole

The South Pole

The other name for the North Pole is the Arctic.

The hottest place on the Earth is called the Equator.

Where is the coldest place on Earth?

Penguins live in the South Pole.

Polar bears live in the North Pole.

Where do you think the hottest place is?

The other name for the South Pole is Antarctica.

'Dough corner' and 'clay square'

LEARNING INTENTIONS

Children will:

- discover that some materials come from natural sources but others are made;

- understand that materials are used for different purposes and have different properties;

- handle malleable materials and begin to relate their activity to the 'real world.'

- discover through play that several processes are involved in making products.

YOU WILL NEED

- modelling clay, dough or plasticine

- rolling pins

- paint

- card

- objects to put in shops

- biscuits

STARTING POINTS

- Make a picture map of the nearest shopping street to the school or nursery. Mark on the places where you can buy things made of dough or clay. Are they 'on a corner' or 'in a square' or 'in the middle' of a street?

- Visit a baker's shop or look in the window of a pottery or china shop.

- Bring in a selection of bread, rolls, cakes and biscuits to form a display. Ask children to copy some of these when playing with playdough.

- Display an assortment of pots and plates. Add labels and enquiry questions such as: 'What is this used for?' 'What picture is on this plate?' 'Find out where this was made.'

CAROL WATSON & COLIN KING

THE TOWN

USBORNE PICTURE WORD BOOKS

Car park

High Street

Mr Brown -the baker

Miss Silver -jeweller

Mr Pa... Mini-market

The Square

Mrs Potts china shop

Stopp and sons - butcher

Post Office

Mr and Mrs Flower fruit and vegetables

Activities

Making models

✋ Give children pieces of soft, self-drying clay, Plasticine or playdough and ask them to create their own object. They explain to an adult how they made it and what it should be used for. When dry it can be painted and/or varnished. A label explaining its use should be put near the product on the display table.

✋ Ask children to make a clay name plaque which they decorate and paint.

Manipulating with hands.

Rolling out the clay.

Painting to finish off.

✋ Make a collection of everyday objects. Talk about the materials used to make them. Add shapes made from paper and ask the children to match them to the objects.

Activities

👐 Take photographs and find pictures of things in your area which are made from clay such as chimney pots, roof tiles, flowerpots and vases, name plaques. Display these on a board above a table on which children's own clay creations are placed.

👐 Find pictures in books and on CD Roms showing ways in which clay is used in other countries such as cooking pots, clay ovens, fine china, houses, bricks. Talk about these and add the pictures to the display.

👐 Make a collection of pictures or find actual examples of house, street and village name plaques. Ask questions such as: 'What is this made from?' 'Is it made from clay?' 'How is it decorated?' 'What colours are used?' 'Where is this sign found?'

👐 Bring in an interesting plate. Explain why you like the plate, where it came from or the story behind it. Ask children to bring in a plate from home (or a picture or drawing of one) and tell the story of where it came from and anything interesting they can find out about it.

👐 Collect objects which would be sold in the shops which are found in the picture map (page 36).

A bowl by Billy age 3 years

Baking

Make biscuits and cakes with different coloured playdough or actual ingredients.

Show children the ingredients used to make bread dough and talk, in simple terms, about the bread making process. Discuss the different sorts of bread you can buy in a shop.

Children make their own roll using prepared dough. This could be taken home with the cooking instructions.

Playdough Recipe - mix in pan. Medium heat until mixture leaves side of pan. Knead. Store in container in fridge.
- Two cups plain flour
- One cup salt
- Two cups water
- Two tablespoons cooking oil
- Two teaspoons cream of tartar
- Add colourings.

Warning! Do not use blue powder paint as it reacts to form a sulphurous gas.

Surveys

Conduct a survey to discover which biscuits or cakes the children like to eat.

Display this information with a small picture or the name of each child in the section showing the picture of their favourite biscuit.

Home Links

- Ask children to look for plates with pictures on them to bring into class to form a display.

- Assist an adult to make biscuits or cakes.

- Look for ways of using clay in and around the home.

- When shopping with parents, look for different sorts of bread, biscuits and cakes which are for sale.

range e 3 years

A snail and pot by Megan

circ

uare

A bridge we saw on holiday by Madison · age 3

On the farm

LEARNING INTENTIONS

Children will:

- gain a greater understanding of farm life;
- know where milk comes from;
- know the difference between physical features and human features;
- develop mapwork skills - plan view.

YOU WILL NEED

- picture sequence of the story of milk
- stories and rhymes about farming
- small pictures of natural features e.g. hill, river, stream
- small pictures of built features e.g. home, road, fence
- coloured card, tissue, paint, shiny paper, glue

STARTING POINTS

- Look at pictures of rural life.
- Take the children on a visit to an 'open farm' if possible.
- Talk about farm products.
- Sing songs such as 'Old MacDonald had a farm'.

Activities

Story sticks

Retell a process such as the story of milk.

You could use story sticks. Draw pictures for the children to sequence.

Put a picture of each stage of the process on a stick and hold each up as you 'tell the story'.

For example:

1. The cow is in the field.
2. She eats the grass.
3. The cow makes milk inside her.
4. The farmer takes the cow to be milked.
5. The machine takes the milk from the cow's udder.
6. The milk goes into a big tank.
7. The tanker takes the milk to the dairy where the milk is put into bottles and containers.
8. We buy milk to use for drinking and cooking.

Repeat with another set of story sticks that enable the children to retell another process on the farm e.g. the story of bread or the story of butter.

The story of milk

Home Links

- Encourage the parents to talk to the children about the processes that take place before the food arrives on the table. Many children when asked 'where does bread come from?' will say 'the shop'.

- Parents can also talk about where the food they eat comes from for example banana plantations in the West Indies, orange groves in Africa etc.

Make a class collage

- Label physical features e.g. rivers, streams, hills.
- Label human features e.g. houses, barns, fences.
- Label animals.
- Write questions on the display as discussion points.

On the farm display:
Some things on the farm are made by people. These are human features.
What can you see on the farm?
Some things are natural. These are physical features.
Which things are made by people? Which things are natural?

On The Farm

Labels: fence, house, haystack, barn, hills, valley, sheep, field, cows, Farmer, Wife, pond, horses, stable, bridge, drive, corn, river, chickens, road, tractor

"...and on the farm he had a ......"

Games to make

Picture / plan matching game
Match the plans of things on the farm to the pictures.
Add labels to the plans.

Physical / human features sorting game
Children put the pictures in the correct set.

Labels: house, fence, haystack, tractor, barn
These are plan views of things found on the farm.
Do you know what they are? Can you label them?

fence, house, Human Features, Which of the pictures are of human features and which are of physical features., Physical Features (natural), barn, river, hills and mountains, road

The world of fairy tales

LEARNING INTENTIONS

Children will:

- retell familiar stories.
- make up their own stories and take part in role play with increasing confidence.
- develop mapwork skills.

Using puppets

YOU WILL NEED

- felt to make finger puppets
- paper plates, bags, old socks
- toys
- paint
- felt tips
- paper

STARTING POINTS

- The children play with puppets and soft toys.
- Ana adult reads or tells a story to be acted out by the children using puppets.

- Use nursery rhymes and stories that have geographical opportunities e.g., 'Golidlocks and The Three Bears', 'Little Red Riding Hood', 'Mary Had A Little Lamb'.

Activities

Stories and rhymes

✋ Using finger puppets depicting familiar characters, children retell the story or the rhyme such as 'Little Red Riding Hood' or 'Two Little Dicky Birds'.

✋ They make appropriate actions in retelling their story to show movement and use geographical vocabulary as applicable such as: 'up the hill' 'across the river' 'through the town' 'round the roundabout' 'over the sea'.

✋ Match the story titles or rhymes to the sets of finger puppets.

✋ Use puppets to act out a story which children have made up with the help of an adult.

✋ Give each child a toy or a puppet. An adult tells them a story involving a series of actions using their own toy or puppet. The adult then asks the children to carry out a series of instructions using the puppets such as:

1. Go down a road
2. Pass through a gate
3. Climb over a wall
4. Look for a house
5. Go in and up the stairs
6. Find a bed and go to sleep

✋ Draw a picture map of the area where the story takes place. Use locational language.

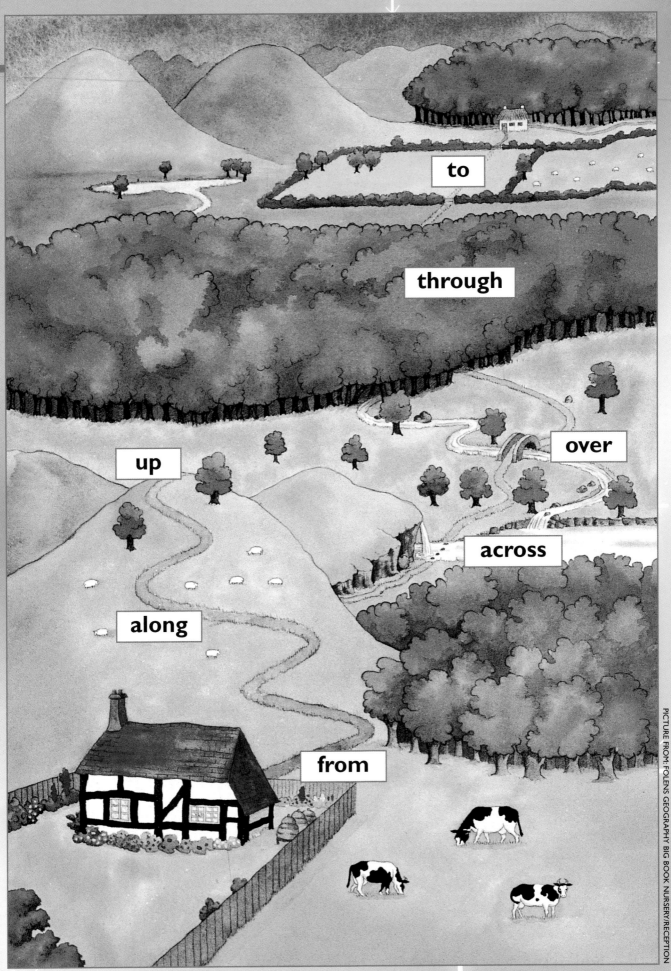

to

through

over

up

across

along

from

Jack and the Beanstalk

Journeys

Some fairy tales are ideal for developing the children's understanding of journeys and their ability to use locational language.

Activities

Tell the story of 'Jack and the Beanstalk'.

- Ask the children to describe Jack's home and the Giant's castle

- Compare the two homes. Encourage the children to use comparatives such as bigger, smaller, larger, longer.

- Talk about the different journeys Jack made:
  - to the market,
  - up the Beanstalk,
  - to the Giant's castle.

Three Billy Goats Gruff

Which way to the green grass?

Can you give the correct directions to get the goats across the bridge?

Go slowly down the hill James

through

Cross over the bridge next to the Troll's house to eat some grass Joshua

Watch out for the warning signs!

Don't go next to the troll Emily

far away

off

in

Close near down

Be careful over the bridge Oliver

Carefully cross over the bridge Mitchell

right

Go slowly to the other side Nathan

on out

Left

straight

The Troll's house is next to the green field Anaba

under

The troll lives under the bridge Samiya

behind

Can you use the characters to make a play? – What directions will you give?

Don't go near the water James

Don't fall off the bridge Sophie

Don't go behind the Troll's door Emily

next to

over

up

Don't go in the water Jack

Don't go through the troll's door Mohsen

Don't go in the house Izabella

Tell the story of 'Three Billy Goats Gruff'

- Ask the children to use locational words to describe the route the goats take.

- Scribe sentences for the children for the display.

- Make small pictures of the characters so that the children can devise a play.

Hansel and Gretel

Lost in the dark

These light sources could help Hansel and Gretel to see in the dark . . . .

A candle

The sun

A torch

A fire

Can you help Hansel and Gretel find their way home?

Over the bridge

Up the path

In front of the fir trees

Across the stream

Behind the tall trees

Past the stump

Over the fence

Tell the story of 'Hansel and Gretel' *Links with geography and science*

- The display above shows a night scene for the journey the children make.

- Talk about how the children will find their way during the day and at night.

- How could a map help them?

- Make a simple map of the area (as on page 42). Laminate it so children can draw the route with a water-based felt tip pen.

LEARNING INTENTIONS

Children will:

- know the various features that make up a town;

- know what services are provided in the town;

- be introduced to north, east, south and west.

STARTING POINTS

- Provide play mats and play maps, homemade and commercially produced, that show roads and rail tracks. These can be used for the children to build on and when playing with toy vehicles. In this way children will learn to follow routes and to build structures in sensible places.

- Play a game such as 'Where does it land?' using something to be rolled on the play mat. Children answer questions such as *Has it landed on a safe place? What feature has it landed on? What would you do there?* This game could be played on a map depicting any environment - country scene, a farm, a large map depicting land and sea.

- Read an information book about the town.

- Play board games, which involve taking turns and moving an object a number of places.

Compass Town board game

- Explain that the children are going to make a game - a pictorial map of an imaginary town.

- Ask the children what buildings they think should go on their game.

- Give them small pieces of paper to draw features of a town.

- Draw roads that run north, east, south and west. Divide the roads into squares and explain to the children that one square equals one move.

- The children should decide where the features should be placed on the board.

- The game can be played at two levels:

Following directions

- Make cards that involve children moving along the board. You can vary the number of instructions according to the ability of the children. You may wish to make a board game that deals only with numbers of less than five for example.

Giving directions

- Make a number of cards that ask the children a direction question.

- Children describe the directions as they move the toy vehicle.

Go 9 squares east, 4 squares south, 5 squares west, 2 squares south.

Where are you?

Go 9 squares east, 1 square north, 7 squares east.

Where are you?

Go 9 squares east, 6 squares south, 5 squares east.

Where are you?

Go 9 squares east, 9 squares south.

Where are you?

Compass Town

Labels on the display:
Which building is east of the cinema?
Where is the train station?
Which building is south of the mosque?
Which buildings are on West Lane?
mosque
North Road
houses
fruit shop
West Lane
flower shop
petrol station
East Street
cinema
hotel
school
train station
church
Which direction would you walk in to get from the houses to the school?
Which buildings are on North Road?
car park
South Drive

Activities

✍ Provide a set of labels with appropriate vocabulary such as *house, road, shop, school, railway station, and car park*. Read the labels with the children and ask them to place the labels in the right place on the class map. Children can use these during undirected play.

✍ Make small cardboard arrows for the children to use with the class map or on a play mat. They plot a route with the arrows for a friend to follow. Use these using some of the conventions such as *stopping at road junctions, driving on the appropriate side of the road*.

✍ Children can make up rhymes to help them remember the four compass points:

For example:

Never Eat Shredded Wheat
Naughty Elephants Squirt Water

Naughty
Elephants
Squirt
Water

Asking questions

In which direction would you walk to get from the flower shop to the school?

Which buildings are north of West Lane?

In which direction would you drive from the fruit shop to the petrol station?

Home Links

Ask parents to:

● Look at maps with their children when going on journeys and use terms like:

We are travelling north to see Grandma. We are going south to London.

● Point out direction signs that give directions and show the miles or kilometres to a destination.

The street where you live

LEARNING INTENTIONS

Children will:

- know where they live;

- be able to count and recognise numbers in the environment;

- increase their awareness that numbers are used in a variety of ways to give information;

- understand that different activities take place in the local area;

- know why different street furniture is used.

YOU WILL NEED
- card
- tissue paper
- paint
- glue
- sugar paper

STARTING POINTS

- Talk to the children about where they live. Do they know their address? Who lives in their home? Ask them to draw a picture of their home with the people who live there. They should add their name to their picture.

- On another piece of paper of the same size as their picture ask them to paint a door. And put the number of their home on it. The door is then cut out on three sides so that it will open. The door is attached to the picture so that, when opened, it reveals the family that lives there.

- Make a group of these pictures into a display with the title 'Who lives here?' Open the doors to find out.

Where do we live?

Activities

Using the environment

- Count how many doors of each colour there are on a building or in a street.

- Do a traffic count identifying colours or types of vehicles passing the building or those found in the car park.

- Use a range of methods to count and display the results. Counting methods could include making a mark on paper or a small chalk or white board, simple tallying, counting aloud and tape recording the voice, using cubes or counters.

Asking questions

Who lives here?

Who lives at number…?

How many people live at number…?

In which house do most people live?

Which house has the smallest family?

Which is your home?

The street where you live

What street furniture can you see?

Ordering numbers

Which is your house?

What number house has a post box outside it?

Can you think why we need to have street lights?

Which side of the road must cars drive on in this country?

What is a 'Give Way' sign for?

In a normal road, there is a house for each number. The numbers alternate on each side of the road. Can you think why they do this?

BUS STOP

Why are there traffic lights by the zebra crossing?

Can you put these number cards in the right order? (some are missing!)

Which gardens have ponds with fish in them?

- Results may be displayed using pictograms, bar charts, computer generated graphs or 3D models.

- Go for a walk in the local area and take photographs to put into a class street book.

- Make a class collage which shows the route you took and where the photographs were taken.

- Make up a story of numbers in the street.

- Ask children to draw a picture of themselves and put in a display of the type of road they live in e.g. road, street, drive, lane

Home Links

Ask parents to:

- Look at the names of the roads and the numbers on buildings with their child when they are out and about.

- Help their child draw three buildings they pass on the way to school.

ROAD	STREET	DRIVE	LANE

The world where we live

LEARNING INTENTIONS

Children will:

- understand that the local area is part of a region;
- know the country in which they live;
- be aware of the wider world;
- recognise different scale maps;
- know that people pollute their environment.

YOU WILL NEED

- waste materials such as paper, cardboard boxes, tubes, fabric
- paint
- coloured paper
- Aerial photograph of the school
- globe
- map of the country
- map of the world

STARTING POINTS

- Talk with the children sensitively and at an appropriate level about some environmental issues. Introduce new vocabulary such as recycle, danger, smoke, waste, pollution.

- Encourage the children to ask their own questions and show care and concern for the environment.

Where do we live?

What jobs do people do?

Factory

Hospital

Doctor

Where do we play?

Paramedic

Nurse

Traffic Warden

Where do people work?

We Live in

High Street

Shops

Shop Assistant

Where do we shop?

Office

Policeman

Fire

High Wycombe

Postman

Teacher

Playground

Town Centre

Fire-fighter

Tesco's

Supermarket

Activities

✋ Ask the children to make models out of some of the waste material you have collected.

✋ Make a Recycling display with the children's models.

✋ Talk about places they have been outside the locality including when they have travelled to other countries to visit relatives or for holidays.

✋ Use the world map to identify places they know or know of because of TV for example.

✋ Use arrows to link their display of the locality to

- the region
- the country
- to the continent
- the globe

Home Links

Encourage parents to collect paper, bottles, and cans and take them to a recycling depot.

Where in the world?

LEARNING INTENTIONS

Children will:

- look at a globe and countries of the world;

- increase their awareness of crafts and traditions in their own and other cultures;

- explore and use natural and manufactured materials in an imaginative and creative way.

YOU WILL NEED

- selection of signs of places

- selection of artefacts from around the world

- tissue to make garlands

- beads to make gifts

- maps

First Atlas

Challenge!
Look at the globe and the atlas

Can you find Great Britain?

Which country is to the south of Great Britain?

Which ocean is to the west of Great Britain?

STARTING POINTS

- Listen to a talk or watch a video about a visit to another country. Talk about the customs which are special to that country.

- Provide a range of artefacts or toys from different parts of the world that are made from different materials.

- Provide examples of nursery, school, village or town signs. Make a school sign; this could be small or large as the one below.

- Provide atlases, globes and photographs for the children to look at.

Activities

Patterns and Signs

In some countries, for example in India, patterns are drawn on the floor outside the door to welcome people into homes. Ask children to design and make their own 'welcome to our class' patterns. These could be made on paper using a range of materials or made in sand or drawn with chalks on paving stones or on washable floor surfaces.

Welcome

✋ Provide examples of gifts which are presented to visitors when they arrive in some places, such as a welcome garland or a hair decoration. Provide the materials for children to make their own versions.

✋ Ask children to design and make a gift they would like to give to a visitor to their class. The examples below are of necklaces the children have made.

✋ Make labels for an artefact display. These could include the names of the artefacts, their country or place of origin, the material they are made from or what they are used for.

✋ Play a game with a set of artefacts, for example one where an adult gives clues without naming the object; children guess what is being described. Another game could involve removing one or two objects from a set of artefacts and the children work out what is missing.

Home Links

● Ask parents to find things in the home which have been made or bought in other countries and talk to their children about them.

● Collect postcards from different places. If parents go on holiday ask them to send the class a postcard.

Where should we go?

Activities

- ✍ Introduce children to a character such as a toy bear who is to go on holiday.
- ✍ Bring in or make a case for the clothes and other items to be taken.
- ✍ Show a map and tickets for travelling.
- ✍ Children try to work out where the bear is going from the objects e.g., a hot or cold place.
- ✍ Talk about where he or she is going and ask questions such as: *'How will he or she get to …?' 'What will he do there?' 'What does she need to pack?'*

TALK ABOUT

Questions to ask	Language development
Where is he going?	Names of places.
How will she get there?	Types of transport.
What will he do there?	Different activities.
What does she need to take?	Clothes, phrase book, sun creams etc.
What type of money will he need?	Introduce different currencies.

- ✍ Children bring in their own toy with a small bag or case already packed.
- ✍ Friends then ask questions to discover the destination.

Activities

- Children select a place on a globe or map of Europe or the World. Describe the things they might see or experience on a journey to that place.

- Display postcards around a map. The example below is of Europe but this could be of one country or another continent.

- Ask and answer questions about the postcards and the countries they are from.

- Display dolls from different countries in traditional costumes. Talk about how traditional dress is different from the ordinary clothes people wear and the reasons people wear traditional costumes.

May 9th is Europe Day

Europe

Europe is a fascinating continent because it includes such a large number of different cultures and countries. Some of the countries are huge, like Russia, the largest country in Europe, and some tiny, such as Andorra. The smallest independent country in the world is the Vatican City in Rome, Italy, which is the headquarters of the Roman Catholic Church.

Can you guess which doll came from Spain?

We have collected postcards and dolls from different countries in Europe.

There are three dolls from Finland.

The doll from Italy has a picture on her apron.

Do you know which dolls have come from Holland?

Faraway places

Activities

- Weaving and sewing.

- Collect examples of goods made with materials which have been woven or plaited such as a basket, a seat cover, piece of cloth, a rug or some hair. Use strips of coloured paper, cloth or wool to weave a pattern to make a small mat or picture.

- Provide a set of simple outline pictures of photographs cut from magazines or old calendars which have been laminated. Punch holes at regular intervals. Ask children to sew these with large blunt needles or laces, choosing appropriate colours. Ask questions about the pictures which may show features of the natural and made environment such as a hill, river, house, car.

- Collect pictures of distant places from calendars, post cards, greeting cards, magazines, or download from the internet.

56

Activities

- Make an artefact display.

- Make labels. These could include the names of the objects, the place they come from, the materials they are made of and what they are used for.

- Play a game with a set of artefacts. The adult gives clues without naming the object. Children guess what it is. Another game could involve removing one or two objects from the display and the children work out what is missing.

- Make a huge display of a distant place. The example shown below is of a rainforest but it could be a desert, the banks of the River Nile, a tropical beach.

- Encourage children to use appropriate vocabulary to describe the features.

- Talk about the similarities and differences of the places they know.

- Ask children to paint giant leaf shapes, suspend these from the ceiling or on the collage

- Hang these at different heights and talk about which is the highest / lowest, biggest / smallest.

We found out about rainforests

lovely magical wonderful special valuable beautiful

Jobs people do

LEARNING INTENTIONS

Children will:

- take part in role-play with confidence and increasing understanding;

- develop their awareness of the jobs people do and the activities people engage in both within and beyond their experience;

- experience a range of cultures and investigate similarities and differences.

STARTING POINTS

- Provide a set of toy figures doing various jobs and talk about the clothes they are wearing and the jobs they do.

- Show pictures which demonstrate people doing different jobs such as the police or farmers.

- Introduce vocabulary such as job, work, uniform, special clothes.

- Invite in a visitor such as a firefighter or a chef to talk to the children about the work they do.

- Read a story or an information book that is about work people do. This could be factual or fictional such as 'The Jolly Postman'; or 'The Lighthouse Keeper's Lunch'.

Activities

Using dressing up clothes

Use your collection of dressing up clothes and equipment to form a display.

Ensure the clothes reflect a range of jobs which can be role-played by both sexes.

Role play: doctors and nurses

Display pictures showing work clothes being worn in real life situations. Provide a set of names of jobs or roles which the children can match to the clothes and/or pictures such as farmer, doctor, shop assistant, child minder, teacher, cook, fire-fighter, priest, disc jockey, police officer, taxi driver.

The children can choose freely which role they wish to assume or the teacher can direct them to a certain role and ask the children to select the appropriate item or items to wear or use. Provide a full-length mirror at child height to encourage discussion.

Adults can participate in the role-play and model behaviour and language which the children learn from.

Put a selection of picture books near the dressing up clothes to give children ideas for play. Change these regularly.

Asking questions

Who wears this?

What is this used for?

Where might I see this?

What would I do with this?

What work does this person do?

Role play: fishing

Home Links

- Ask children to bring in pictures from magazines or books to add to the collection of people working in another country.

- Ask parents and carers to talk to the children about:

  – the work they do.

  – the work people do in the places they visit e.g. leisure centre, supermarket, cinema, hospital

Role play: cafe

Role play: a Vietnamese meal

Role play: gardens

In the playground and park

LEARNING INTENTIONS

Children will:

- know more about signs and symbols and use these in free and directed play;
- follow oral and printed directions;
- be aware of why and how people can take care of the environment;
- know what people do in the park.

YOU WILL NEED

- wheeled toys
- paint
- stipple paint brushes
- paper
- paint
- straws
- glue

STARTING POINTS

- Children play on pedal cars, bicycles, trikes and other wheeled toys.
- Children play in an open space, playground or park.
- Talk about the children's experiences of visiting parks.

- Read the children a story or a poem such as 'After the Storm'. Use the book to introduce new vocabulary for example *storm, wind, fence, tree, branch, roots, stream, bridge, lake, acorn*.

Activities

Signs and symbols

- Talk about and make some symbols that children already know such as stop, go, no entry, traffic lights, pedestrian crossing. Children can use these in outdoor play activities.

- Make sets of cards with directions for children to use in the playground such as symbols, arrows, numerals and number symbols.

- Make cards for children to follow a route around the large apparatus. These may use words and phrases such as; *go under, climb over, walk through* or you may use picture clues, which the children have already been taught.

Activities

- Devise with the children a 'Code of conduct in the park'.

- Make a list (teacher may scribe) of ways children can improve the park environment. Talk about putting litter in bins, not picking flowers, not pulling on branches, the importance of playing in safe places.

- Make a class collage of 'Fun in the park'. Children can paint pictures of activities they can do in the park or of features they might find there.

- Children can make 3-D models of park playground furniture with straws.

- Children can make mosaic type pictures by using paint and a stipple technique.

Home Links

Ask parents to:

- Look with their children for signs and symbols in the environment and to explain their meaning.

- Visit a local park and help their child draw pictures of what they did there.

Harry, Amna and Syed made the roundabouts.

Euella, Jack and Luc made the see-saw.

Rose's slide

Rose and Ashley made the swing.

Iqra, Georgina and Olivia made this climbing frame.

Fun in the park

in
above
up
near
down
outside
off
below
next to
beside
by
in
under
at
in front
along
behind
across

Action songs and rhymes

YOU WILL NEED

- paint and brushes
- tissue paper
- material
- coloured pencils
- glue
- card

LEARNING INTENTIONS

Children will:

- begin to understand that they are singing and talking about songs and rhymes that relate to the world around them;
- ask and answer questions;
- develop an awareness of environmental issues.

In all cases it is expected that you would sing the song a number of times so the children become familiar with it.

- Sing action songs and rhymes that relate to the real world.
- Use something which the children have created which relates to a song or rhyme such as a bus for 'The wheels on the bus go round and round' or the log and pool scene for 'Five little speckled frogs' or the pan and sausages for 'Ten fat sausages'.

Five Little Ducks

1 2 3 4 5

- Make a picture to show where the ducks went.
- Make ducks to move around the picture. These can be given names or letters or numbers and used for word, letter and number recognition.
- Cut out duck shapes from card for the children to decorate with material, paper, feathers.
- Punch holes in the shapes for threading or sewing.
- Provide a set of laminated labels for the children to attach to the picture in the right place using Blutack or Velcro pieces. These could include:

  - *over the hills*
  - *up the hill*
  - *along the path*
  - *through the wood*
  - *across the river*
  - *in the water.*
  - *over the stepping stones*

- Talk about what the ducks would see, what they would pass, what food they would eat, who they would meet.
- Ask questions such as: 'If you went swimming, where would you go? What would you wear?' 'Why must you be careful near water?'

5 little ducks went swimming one day.........

........over the hills and far away.

One little duck went swimming one day over the hills and far away. He was having so much fun he asked another one to come. Two little ducks went swimming one day ....

Five little speckled frogs

Five little speckled frogs
sat on a speckled log
eating a most enormous grub
YUM YUM
One fell into the pool
where it was nice and cool
then there were four speckled frogs
GLUB GLUB
Four little speckled frogs
sat on a speckled log
eating.......

5 little speckled frogs

1
2
3
4
5

👋 Draw, or place, cut out card or cloth log and pool shapes on the floor for children to act out the song. Talk about the story which the song tells explaining the words used.

👋 Make a collage picture of the scene for the five speckled frogs. Use cut out frogs or felt frog finger puppets for the children to move as appropriate.

👋 Talk about the different environments and habitats which may surround the log and the pool. Introduce vocabulary such as mud, stones, reeds. Ask children to imagine what it would feel like to be in the different locations such as: 'in the pool' 'on the log' 'under the stone' 'in the mud' 'among the reeds'.

👋 Make a cardboard wheel with a spinner to use with your collage picture. Divide the wheel into sections with an instruction such as 'put one frog in the mud' in each section. Children take turns to spin and follow the instruction.

Home Links

● Send home a list of words which have been introduced as new vocabulary and ask parents to use these, where possible, in general conversations with their child.

● Look for examples of some of the words such as wall, bus, star, hill, log. Draw a picture of one of them.

Books in the Belair series

Language
- Language in Colour
- Language on Display
- Legend into Language
- On First Reading
- Paint a Poem
- Patchwork of Poems
- Rainbow Year
- Sounds Interesting
- Sounds Like This
- Tell Me a Tale
- Turning the Page
- Words with Wings

Maths
- A Number of Things
- Maths on Display
- Numeracy on Display
- The Maths Collection

Science
- Discoveries
- The Art of Science

Humanities
- A Sense of Place
- Picture the Past
- Starting with Me
- Time for Reflection

Information Technology
- Creative Computing
- Developing Art through IT

Cross-curricular
- A World of Display
- Collections
- Creative Elements
- Display for all Seasons
- Enterprising Ideas
- Hands on Display
- In a Moment
- Storyline Topics
- Tales for Topics

Art and Craft
- Art in Focus
- Art of Different Cultures
- Art of Recycling
- Art for Writing
- A Work of Art
- Collections
- Material Pleasures
- In the Picture
- Outstanding Art
- Puppet Talk
- Simply Artistic
- Something Special
- Starting Points in Art
- You've been Framed

Music, Dance and Drama
- Just Imagine
- Music Works
- Time to Dance (book)
- Time to Dance (cassette)

Food and Cookery
- The Spice of Life

P.S.H.E.
- A Positive Approach

Assembly
- Time for Reflection

The Little Bell series
- Creative Christmas
- Let's Make a Book

Belair Early Years
- Art
- I.C.T
- Music
- Our World
- Stories
- Waterplay